Walking TALL

how to build confidence and be the best you can be

Walking TALL

how to build confidence and be the best you can be

by Marie-José Auderset
illustrated by Gaëtan de Séguin
edited by N. B. Grace

sunscreen

Library of Congress Cataloging-in-Publication Data:
Auderset, Marie-José.
Walking tall : how to build confidence and be the best you can be /
by Marie-José Auderset ; illustrated by Gaëtan de Séguin ;
edited by N.B. Grace.
p. cm. — (Sunscreen)
Includes bibliographical references and index.
ISBN 978-0-8109-9479-9 (alk. paper)
1. Self-confidence. 2. Adolescent psychology. I. Séguin, Gaëtan de. II.
Grace, N. B. III. Title.
BF575.S39A93 2008
158.1—dc22
2007043416

Translated by Gita Daneshjoo

Book series design by Higashi Glaser Design

Printed and bound in China
10 9 8 7 6 5 4 3 2 1

HNA ▌▌▐▐▐
harry n. abrams, inc.
a subsidiary of La Martinière Groupe
115 West 18th Street
New York, NY 10011
www.hnabooks.com

contents

phase 2: MY FAMILY AND ME

phase 3: ME AND OTHERS

NOBODY UNDER-
STANDS ME
I CAN'T DO ANY-
THING RIGHT
I WISH I HAD
MORE FRIENDS
I'M NOT GOOD
ENOUGH

Self-confidence may seem like a small thing, but having self-esteem—or *not* having it—can completely change your life! When you have it, you feel like you can move mountains. When you don't, it seems impossible to overcome the smallest obstacle.

Fortunately, just because you feel shy and awkward today doesn't mean that you won't feel good about yourself in the future. Self-confidence takes time to develop, and it grows when you learn to pay attention to how you really feel.

That sounds simple, but it's not always so easy. This book will help you understand what happens inside when you experience feelings of self-doubt. It will give you pointers on how to feel more at ease in various situations, and how to believe in yourself. As you try out these tips, you'll find that you're developing more self-confidence every day!

being loved for who you are

WE'RE ALL THE SAME—

you're great! (but sometimes you forget)

exercise your rights!

here's always a first time . . .

celebrities aren't that different from us

AND WE'RE ALL DIFFERENT

Ah! Here it is!

where does low self-esteem come from?

riding the
self-confidence
roller coaster

One day, you feel good about yourself: you can defend your point of view in an argument without getting upset, you can tell your friends a story and make them laugh, you like the way you look, and you feel pretty smart. Basically, you like yourself.

The next day, though, you may doubt yourself: you focus only on your weaknesses, you feel like you don't quite measure up to others when it comes to your intelligence or athletic ability, and, of course, you *hate* your looks. You might even feel like you hate yourself.

What causes this sudden shift from feeling okay to feeling as if you should lock yourself in your room for the next decade or so?

As you probably know from experience, it doesn't take much for your self-esteem to plummet. Read through the following situations and imagine how you'd feel if they happened to you:

- You stumble over your words while giving a presentation, even though you learned it by heart.
- You blush when someone looks at you.
- You feel stupid when asked a question.
- You don't want to go to gym class because you're afraid people will make fun of you.
- During breaks at school, you go off on your own rather than hang out with other people.
- You lie on your bed daydreaming rather than tackling a project that interests you.
- You avoid being called on when your teacher asks for volunteers for an activity, even though you think you would enjoy it.

- You feel ugly when people look at you.
- You think that even if someone is interested in you, he or she will be disappointed once they get to know you better.

It's as though you had a little angel on one shoulder and a little devil on the other. When you think of trying something new or striking up a conversation with someone you don't know well, the angel smiles and whispers in your ear, "Go for it, you can do it!" The devil, on the other hand, looks very serious and asks, "What if you don't succeed? What will people think?"

If you listen to the little devil, your self-confidence falls apart. Unfortunately, there may be many days when the devil seems to be making a lot of sense. Fortunately, you can learn how to shut him out and pay attention to the angel instead. Once you do that, you'll become a more assertive, confident person.

That may sound impossible to you right now, but if you practice some of the ideas presented in this book, you will gradually change until one day you feel ready to take on the world.

what does
high self-esteem
look like?

Having high self-esteem means having confidence in yourself, thinking positively about what you say and do, and loving yourself unconditionally. That sounds great—but how does that translate into everyday life? Here are some clues:

I'm measuring my self-esteem . . .

Nick, what are you doing with my tape measure?

If you have *confidence in yourself*, it means you know that you're capable of doing your best. For example, a teen named Lucy says, "When I find myself in an unexpected situation, I try to find a good way to deal with it. I trust myself. Even if I'm in a tough situation, panicking won't get me anywhere."

If you *think positively about yourself*, you know that whatever you do or say has meaning, even if you make mistakes. "When someone criticizes me," says Joanne, "I try to understand where they're coming from. If I did something wrong, I try to find a way to make it better. Otherwise, I explain my side of the story."

If you *love yourself unconditionally*—despite your flaws, weaknesses, and failures—you will respect yourself and pay attention to your needs. "When I'm fighting with one of my friends and realize the situation is getting the best of me," admits Alicia, "I often feel the need to be alone." She doesn't ignore that feeling. Instead, she goes to her room and spends some time by herself until she calms down.

Do you want to figure out how much self-esteem you have? Here's a quick checklist:

☑ You accept yourself as you are. Of course, you have goals that you want to reach and ways that you want to improve yourself, but you've also learned how to be content with where you are right now.

☑ You are daring enough to try new things.

☑ You know what your strengths and weaknesses are, and you're willing to try to fix your faults.

☑ You take pride in what you do.

☑ You recognize your right to be happy.

☑ You don't always agree with others, and you're not afraid to speak up when you disagree with someone. But you're not arrogant and you don't think you have all the answers, either.

where does
low self-esteem
come from?

For a house to withstand wind and rain, it needs a strong foundation and sturdy construction. In the same way, it's easier to have high self-esteem when you have a solid base that has been built up from the time you were born. Every child needs to experience five primary feelings in order to grow up to become a healthy and happy adult:

1. You feel *secure* if you are loved and protected, if you can depend on your loved ones and trust them, if your family life is stable (and not plagued by health problems, unemployment, or psychological problems), and if you don't constantly live in a state of fear or anxiety.

2. You feel *recognized* and *accepted* as you are by your loved ones—

with all your good qualities and shortcomings. If your personality has room to grow within your family, you can learn to freely express your feelings and beliefs.

3.   You feel that you *belong* to a family or a certain way of life. You're surrounded by people who matter to you, and with whom you share a common history.

4.   You feel *confidence* in your academic abilities. This is not about getting good grades and being the star student. It's about knowing that you can learn more each day. It's about recognizing your personal triumphs and not feeling doomed when you make mistakes.

5.   You feel *comfortable* with people of all ages. With good social skills, you don't think twice about approaching new people and getting to know them better. You have friends and are known among your classmates and teachers.

Don't worry if you've encountered difficulties that have prevented you from developing these feelings. You can build your self-esteem at any stage in life. And you can also help it grow faster by changing the way you think.

You'll find that although you can't change reality, you *can* change the way you see yourself. And that makes a huge difference!

Here's an example: Jim had to give a presentation in front of his class. Everything went well, although he did hesitate once or twice and punctuated his speech with plenty of "ums." When he sat down, he could have convinced himself that his presentation was a disaster and that he's worthless. All that hard work down the drain!

Or he could take pride in how much he had learned about his topic and how he was able to tell the rest of the class about what he had discovered. He hasn't forgotten about the problems with his speech, but he grew from the experience and he'll work harder to correct those problems the next time he gives a speech. If this is how he reacts to his performance, it means that he has high self-esteem.

you're great!

(but sometimes you forget)

Having high self-esteem doesn't depend on looks or talent. And it *really* doesn't depend on being perfect—after all, everyone makes mistakes. But if you have good self-esteem, a little voice inside your head always reminds you that you're a worthwhile person, even if you have just messed up.

This little voice is important. It reminds you that you can overcome obstacles. It helps you know what your limits are, so you don't take excessive risks. And even if you fail, it encourages you by saying that the experience will help you learn more about yourself.

However, sometimes you might not hear the little voice in your head. Maybe it's speaking too softly or maybe another, more negative voice has taken its place. Here's what that voice sounds like: *I'll never succeed. I'm just not as good as other people. I'm ugly. I can't do anything right. Nobody loves me. Nobody understands me. I'm worthless.*

These kinds of thoughts are quite powerful. If you don't get rid of them, you may start to feel terrible all the time. Not only will you feel bad, but you'll have a hard time making friends or achieving goals because the voice will have convinced you that you can't.

Because I'm worth it!

Satisfaction Guaranteed!

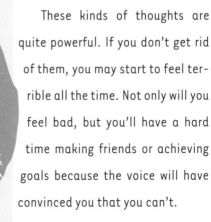

But there is some good news! You can learn to block negative thoughts the moment they begin. Once you learn to stop thinking negatively, you'll find that your outlook on life automatically gets brighter. Here's something to try:

Choose one or two sentences that motivate you and help you believe in yourself, such as: *I am as good as anybody else. I will succeed. I'm smart. I love myself just the way I am. I feel happy and at ease when I'm around people.*

Set aside time every day to repeat these sentences to yourself, either out loud or in your head.

Of course, sometimes these sentences will seem artificial. You may find that you're repeating the words without thinking about what they mean—or even believing them. But keep trying. It takes time to change the way your mind works. Before long, you'll be surprised by how natural it feels to say these positive things to yourself, and you'll begin to realize that you have more confidence.

exercise
your rights!

When you lack self-esteem, you tend to keep to yourself, avoid approaching other people, and try to attract the least attention possible. But you can change that once you develop the mindset that you have as much right as anyone to claim your place in the world.

A couple of psychologists have drawn up a list of rights that may be obvious to some people, but are generally overlooked by those who are less sure of themselves. Read through this list and see how many statements you believe:

I have the right to live.

I have the right to be myself.

I have the right to grow.

I have the right to succeed.

I have the right to act.

I have the right to be important.

I have the right to belong to a family or a group.

I have the right to be close to others and to share with them what I feel.

I have the right to be physically and mentally healthy.

I have the right to think for myself.

I have the right to feel.

I have the right to be a child.

In order to have self-esteem, you need to *believe* that you have these rights and you need to *act* as if you have these rights. If you're feeling a little shaky about some of them, try this: tape the list to your desk or next to your bed and read it from time to time, especially when you experience difficulties or start to doubt yourself. Whatever you do, don't think that you're the only person in the entire world who feels bad about himself or herself. Most people lack confidence from time to time, even if they don't show it.

there's always a
first time . . .

Even successful and famous people sometimes suffer moments of self-doubt and low self-esteem. So imagine how hard it is for someone like you, who is still a teenager and who doesn't have a lot of life experience, to be sure of yourself all the time. After all, your life is a constant list of "first times": first sleepover, first exam, first love, first evening out with your friends . . .

With each new day and each new experience, you gain more independence and freedom. That's great—but, of course, you'll also make mistakes. When that happens, you may wonder whether you can trust yourself to do the right thing or whether others can trust you.

For example, John remembers the first time his parents left him home alone. He had mixed feelings about it: On one hand, he was sure he could handle it; on the other hand, he was worried that he couldn't.

"I was annoyed and angry that they left me with so many instructions and orders," he says. "I spent the whole day with my friends—that part was fine. But at night, I watched a scary movie. I spent the next several hours locked away in my room, listening to the sounds the house was making. I was really scared. I was convinced that there was somebody in the house. When I woke up the next morning, I was embarrassed. I was worried over nothing. It didn't help my self-confidence at all!"

Though such experiences are difficult, living through such "first times" will help you learn how to lead an independent life. You might want to be perfect the first time you do something, but you can learn a lot from your mistakes.

For example, Thea remembers the first time she babysat. She was afraid she wouldn't know what to do. "I relied on the fact that I could call my mother and she was ready to come to my rescue if something went wrong," she recalls. "Today, I have a lot more confidence in myself. I've found that I have an easier handle on new situations."

Think of some situations that made you anxious a few months ago and then think about how you handle them today. You'll probably realize that most of them don't bother you anymore. Remember that when you face your next new challenge!

accept yourself the
way you are

It's hard not to compare yourself to other kids. For example, most young people (and many older ones, too!) are very sensitive about what others think about their looks.

You might worry that your nose is too wide, your ears stick out, you're too short, or your face is covered in acne. Sometimes it may seem that this is all you can think about. When you see yourself in the mirror or catch your reflection in a store window, all you see are the things you hate about your appearance. You blush when people look at you, and you try everything you can think of to hide your hated features. If this sounds like you, then you know that focusing too much on your looks can seriously damage your self-esteem.

For example, Alexandra canceled several trips with friends due to acne breakouts. She simply couldn't bear showing her face. Adam hates the fact that he's only five foot four and tries to think up every imaginable way of putting on a few inches: wearing thick-soled sneakers, standing up straighter, and standing on slight elevations—such as on curbs or steps—when he's with a group.

Rachel says, "With my excess weight, I can't believe that anyone would find me attractive." Sandra goes even further, "No one will love me if I have small breasts." With this kind of thinking, you risk shutting yourself off from other people, which only makes matters worse.

If you feel this way, don't keep it hidden. Discuss your issue with a parent or another adult you trust. Their guidance and advice will help you put the problem in perspective. (And if you think you can't talk to anyone, remember that building up the courage to discuss something that's troubling you already shows that you're becoming a stronger person.)

You can also talk about how you feel with your friends. Ask them if they have similar worries about their looks. Their answers might surprise you. Even those who strike you as charming and confident may say something like: "I hate my feet," "I don't like my teeth," or "I think my eyes are too close together." You'll also probably notice that they are exaggerating their flaws—which should be a hint that you, too, are probably overstating things.

Maggie's face

Sandra's breasts

Louise's hands

Julie's legs

My toes

celebrities
aren't that different from us

Your self-confidence might also take a blow when you're leafing through a celebrity magazine. Most stars are drop-dead gorgeous, with the power to quicken heartbeats. But keep in mind that Brad Pitt, Beyoncé, Orlando Bloom, Jennifer Aniston, and Zac Efron make up less than 1 percent of the population. The rest of us must make do with the face and body we have, and learn to accept and love ourselves as we are.

It's also important to remember that those photos don't usually show how singers, models, athletes, and actors look in real life. The magazine's art staff can use computer software to get rid of an actor's pimples, trim inches off her waist, and even change the color of her hair!

For example, Kate Winslet, who played the lead role in *Titanic*, was watching television and heard a young woman say that she wanted a figure that was as beautiful as Winslet's after seeing Winslet's photo in a magazine. The actress then told the press that, in fact, the photographs had been manipulated to make her body look more attractive.

So the next time you come across photographs of your favorite movie stars, remember that what you see or read isn't always reality.

put me in, coach!

(or, on second thought, don't . . .)

Even though you may accept your face and figure, you may worry about your athletic abilities. Physical activity gives you energy and makes you healthy—that much you know—but before you can reap those benefits, you have to go to the gym.

This is tough if you're not a fan of gym class. Does this description sound like you? You hate running laps, you always drop the ball in softball games, you're scared the volleyball will smash you in the face, and, to top it all off, you're embarrassed to be seen in gym shorts. Maybe your gym teacher ruined it for you early on, when he asked the two most athletic students to pick their teams and you were the last one chosen. Of course, *someone* has to be last, but you may have told yourself that this meant you were no good at sports and you gave up trying.

This is a common reaction among kids who aren't naturally gifted athletes. But even if you'll never make the varsity team or win a marathon, you'll still get all the health benefits of exercising if you do the best you can.

From now on, try to approach sports and exercise with less fear. When it comes to team sports, run, sprint, and throw everything you've got into the game, and don't worry about how well you're doing. Like the world's greatest athletes, you'll increase your stamina and improve your balance and coordination, which will help you feel better about yourself. This new attitude will help you in countless situations—even outside gym class.

If you can, pick a sport that's a good fit for your size, build, skills, and interest. For example, you might enjoy soccer, swimming, or archery more

than wrestling or football. You may have to shop around a bit for an activity you like. As you do so, try to find a sport with more experienced players who are willing to help you, or a coach who seems patient and understanding.

Don't feel you have to pick a popular sport. In fact, the reception and atmosphere of "smaller" sports teams are usually warmer; and your new team members will likely be more tolerant if your performance is less than stellar.

one pound
too many?

Another common difficulty for young people, particularly girls, is the fear of being overweight. If you obsess over a few extra pounds, you likely suffer from body-image problems and low self-confidence. You feel guilty every time you eat, thinking that you've done your body a great disservice.

I lost one pound this week.

I gained five . . .

Like many other kids your age, you've probably made some halfhearted attempts to diet. But if you really do need to lose weight, it's best to consult a doctor or nutritionist. They can help you lose the extra pounds without resorting to starving yourself, which will make you tired and cause other health problems.

If you want to lose a pound or two, avoid traps such as extreme dieting or smoking. Alter your behavior instead: start your day with a good breakfast to avoid mid-morning hunger pangs, eat more fruit and vegetables, control your sugar intake, and avoid sugary drinks and snacks. Don't eat between meals or in front of the television. And practicing a sport gives you even more opportunity to lose those extra pounds and feel better about your body.

the dreaded
dressing room

Buying new clothes can be fun, but it can also present yet another situation where your self-esteem is threatened. When you're in the dressing room, you may try everything you can to look better—sucking in your stomach, tightening your buttocks, standing ramrod straight, smiling at the mirror—but nothing seems to work. Your reflection just doesn't look the way you want it to. You may think, "I'm not pretty enough to get away with this tank top" or "I'm not buff enough to wear these jeans."

You're basically telling yourself that you're ugly because the clothes don't suit you. But think about this: you could also have said, "This shirt is poorly cut" or "These pants are made for a different body type." Take a look at your classmates. Some of them have long legs with a short torso or vice versa. Some have extra weight around their waists; some have heavy thighs. When you take into account all the different kinds of body shapes there are in the world, it's no wonder that every piece of clothing doesn't look good on every figure. So next time you reject a pair of pants in the dressing room, don't blame it on your body. Remember that each body type is unique and focus on finding clothes that flatter you.

write a confidence
checklist

Let's say you do find an outfit that looks good on you. A feeling of elation sweeps over you when you gaze in the mirror. You look more confident, you stand taller, you smile at yourself—you feel great!

Unfortunately, that great outfit won't help if someone makes a mean comment to you at school or you get a bad grade on a test. That's why it's important to take note of your personal strengths—the ones that you'll always have, no matter what you're wearing.

Here's a tip on how to do that:

On the left-hand side of a piece of paper, write a list of your strengths (including what you like about your body, your personality, your mental and physical abilities, and so on). Your list might include items like this: good sense of humor, imaginative, trustworthy, good friend, good at math, willingness to help others, beautiful eyes, strong arms, ability to compromise, curly hair, and so on.

On the right-hand side, write a list of your weaknesses. Put a check mark by the things you can change about yourself (for example, you admit your bedroom isn't very neat, you're always late with your homework, you're a little out of shape, and you get angry easily). That will let you know that these are areas where you can improve, with a little work. If there are things on the list that you can't do anything about, like your ears that stick out or your freckles, then practice accepting them. There's no point in worrying about something you can't change!

You might find your list of flaws to be longer than your list of strengths, but don't worry about that for now. Just put the paper aside.

The next day, look at the paper again and rewrite your list of strengths, adding more now that you've had time to think about your list. Acknowledging your skills, intelligence, and kindness doesn't make you egotistical; it helps you to pinpoint your strengths. And you should be proud of them!

Then ask your friends and family members what qualities they like in you. You'll probably be surprised by some of the answers, and you'll find that you won't see yourself in the same way again.

When negative thoughts or feelings start creeping back, reread your list of strengths. Imagine yourself in situations in which you can put them to use. Though this won't solve all your problems, such positive thinking will keep doubts at bay and help you feel ready to take on the world.

being loved for
who you are

My personality changes depending on whether I feel confident or not. Sometimes I feel sure about myself; when I'm being positive, I don't attach any importance to other people's criticisms of me. I'm full of energy and feel like I could move mountains.

Other times, I'm more negative. I put myself down and stop believing in myself. I lack motivation and imagine myself with every flaw. I can barely carry on a conversation, let alone feel comfortable meeting someone I don't know.

The truth is that it doesn't take a lot for me to start doubting myself and putting myself down. It all depends on whether I'm tired or rested, what kind of mood I'm in, or whether I've just had a fight with my parents or my best friend. They all have an impact on my state of mind. But I'm trying to improve my self-esteem every day. And I know my friends and family really love me for who I am.

—Sophia

my letter of praise

take care of yourself!

confidence at home

MY BROTHER, MY SISTER...
AND ME

ALL FAMILIES are DIFFERENT

**work hard,
play hard**

MY FAMILY
AND ME

family
burdens

all families
are different

You're different from your parents, brothers, and sisters—and you probably let them know it! However, you have shared a life with them from day one, so you're influenced by their behaviors and attitudes toward life. Some families move through life with confidence, taking pride in their ability to adapt to all situations.

For example, Jeanne says, "I envy Ellen. When I visit her family and talk to her mother, I get the sense that she's very sure of herself. She's very assertive. We're much shyer at our house. We're always afraid of stepping on one another's toes."

Members of families who suffer from low self-esteem live in a constant state of anxiety. They feel they might not be strong or competent enough to handle difficult situations, so they prefer to stay in the background. "When someone pays me a compliment," Andrew says, "my dad always responds, 'Stop it. He might end up believing it.' He acts as though compliments are only meant for others. This makes me uncomfortable, not to mention angry."

If your family lacks confidence, it's natural to feel down about it and think that you're going to be the same when you grow up. However, lacking self-confidence also allows you to develop certain positive traits. For example, shy people usually have more finesse when it comes to relationships. They don't try to push other people around. Because they are sensitive to others' reactions, they make good listeners and understand others' problems and difficulties. They are willing to take other people's advice, while people who move through life like a steamroller, unhindered by doubts or uncertainties, often make big mistakes because they're so sure they're right.

But don't let these positive aspects overshadow your quest for more self-assurance. If you boost your self-confidence, you'll have the best of both worlds: you'll be more sure of yourself, while also being sensitive and open to others.

It may help to jot down your feelings in a diary. That's one way of assessing the day's events and organizing your thoughts. Write down the good and the bad things that happened to you and how you reacted to those events. Write down your innermost thoughts. Try to write poetry or draw pictures about what you're feeling. Even writing down negative feelings, like anger or jealousy, will help because you'll get a little distance on what's upsetting you. By taking the time to learn more about yourself, you'll begin to figure out which situations or people help you feel better about yourself and which ones don't.

confidence
at home

Regardless of your level of self-esteem, you probably feel most at ease with your family. You don't need to worry about your image with them because your family loves you and believes in you. Your home is a refuge, where you feel understood.

"I never lack self-confidence at home," Eddie says. "I know that my family understands and appreciates me the way I am. I can really be myself

with them. But it's different at school or around the neighborhood, where people can make fun of me."

It's no surprise that your family's opinion counts a great deal; after all, this feeling of trust was built over the years. As you get older, however, you need independence. Although your parents will remain important fixtures in your life, it's natural for you to veer away from what they do and say at times. You might not always share their outlook; you may want to compare their advice to that of your friends and classmates.

"I need to know where my parents stand on every important issue," Steve says. "It helps me feel secure, even if I don't always follow their advice. Before making a decision, I find out what my parents think and then decide what works best for me."

Distancing yourself from your parents is normal, too, even if it sometimes involves fights and disagreements. But don't worry. Just because you're starting to make your own decisions doesn't mean you're disap-

pointing your parents or losing their love. There's only one way of becoming truly independent: by learning to make your own choices and dealing with the consequences. Each time you think or do something on your own, look at the experience as a small victory that will help you start to believe more in yourself.

If, at some point, things don't go your way or you've made a poor decision, don't beat yourself up about it. Just try again. "When I wanted to take karate, my parents tried to dissuade me," recalls John. "They thought I was involved in too many extracurricular activities. But I was sure I could balance my schoolwork and sports. I insisted so much that they finally let me do it. Two months later, I gave it up. My grades started to suffer because I didn't have enough time to do my homework."

This kind of thing may happen to you, but the fact that you miscalculated or didn't succeed the first time you tried something new shouldn't be interpreted as failure. Use the opportunity to figure out why it didn't work and learn how you can do it better next time. For example, John decided to

go to karate camp during summer vacation. He figured out a way to learn more about a sport he was interested in without jeopardizing his studies—and he also learned more about how much work he could take on.

good grades don't always
make you happy

Even though you might feel confident at home, there is a place where you go nearly every day that has the power to undermine your self-confidence: school. If you get a bad grade—or even a grade that's lower than what you or your parents wanted—things can get a little tense at home. You may start to lose confidence in yourself and your abilities, especially if you think you've disappointed your parents or if they scold you for not having done better.

Your self-esteem suffers even more when they say things such as: "I always said that you weren't applying yourself" or "How can you succeed if you don't give it your all?" If they're particularly annoyed, you might even get grounded.

Of course, it would be ideal if your parents stopped comparing you to other kids and realized that you have to learn at your own speed. Unfortunately, at school—as in society at large—your performance is often judged in comparison with others. Because your mother and father want the best for your future, they may push you to surpass your limitations.

"I was doing poorly in school," Adrienne recalls. "My parents believed in me, and I worked hard all winter long. But by the time spring rolled around, I was exhausted. I would cry over nothing!"

When pressure mounts, you may become stressed, find it hard to concentrate, and make mistakes. You can get caught in a vicious cycle that makes you doubt yourself more and more and prevents you from bringing out the best in yourself.

work hard,
play hard

Striking the right balance between schoolwork and relaxation isn't easy. Try to organize your time so you can finish your work without sacrificing time for chilling out. For example, set aside an hour and a half for homework after school. Afterward, you can do what you want: read, listen to music, or hang out with your friends. These activities will help you ease the tensions of school, and you'll feel recharged when you go back to studying.

Also, think about *how* you work. Do you concentrate enough when you're doing your homework? Is there a way you can be more productive? You may want to ask an adult—your parents, your guidance counselor, or a favorite teacher—for tips on how to study and work more effectively.

If you show your parents that you're doing the best you can, they will probably lighten up a bit. If you still feel stressed out by their expectations, have an honest talk with them and explain that their pressure is actually hurting your efforts to do well in school. And remember: your getting a bad grade in school doesn't mean they love you any less.

This year, math nearly choked me. Now, with my mother's help, things will get easier . . .

remember the

tortoise and the hare...

If school takes up a lot of time in your day-to-day routine, it probably annoys you to know that other kids might work a lot less than you to get the same grades—or even better grades. And if those kids happen to include your brother or sister, it's even worse.

You might think, "It's so unfair. My brother does his homework in half the time it takes me and brings home good grades. It's discouraging. Why, if we came from the same parents, don't I have as good a memory?" Every day, you have to spend more time and energy than your siblings to learn new things. By nighttime, you're exhausted, while they've spent the evening doing whatever they want. You can't stand having to compare yourself to them when report-card time comes around. If you find yourself in this situation, your self-confidence will definitely be put to the test.

But remember this: although it's great to finish homework quickly and have time for fun, it doesn't mean that someone who works more slowly isn't just as smart. Imagine two brothers leaving for a trip. One takes a high-speed train and the other takes a normal one. The first brother will arrive at his destination faster, but he'll have less time to appreciate the scenery. The second brother will see houses, a bird in a tree, a beautiful river. They both saw the landscape, but in very different ways.

When it comes to homework, faster isn't always better. By taking more time to study, you might discover details that escape your brother or sister's attention. You might be better at explaining the exercises to others, because you've taken the time to observe the material from all angles.

Here's another benefit: you'll learn how to work more productively, because you'll want to make the most of each minute. And you'll also know that you have enough energy to stick to a difficult task. It's a true gift to know that. It will allow you to have greater confidence in yourself. Think of that next time you get annoyed that you're still studying while your brother or sister is playing video games. And always remember that even though you might not be the quickest learner, you're still intelligent.

my brother, my sister . . .
and me

School isn't the only point of comparison between siblings. There are probably a lot of differences between you and them, including physical features (who got dad's big nose and who got mom's wavy hair?), the ease with which you meet others (who knows how to make a great impression?), the interest others have shown in you (who gets the most attention?), and your performance in school (who gets the best grades?). When you have high self-esteem, you're not threatened by your siblings' strengths because you know you have many strengths of your own. You like yourself enough that you don't envy them.

On the other hand, if you suffer from low self-esteem, you can't stand making comparisons. "My sister doesn't miss an opportunity to make herself

What happened to you?

I'm allergic to my sister!

noticed," says Kelly. "Everyone loves her. I feel like a little black sheep next to her. I feel like everything I do or say is boring." No wonder arguments can start at the drop of a hat!

"When my sister comes into the kitchen while I'm eating breakfast," Kelly continues, "sometimes all it takes is a whiff of her perfume to get me angry. It annoys me that she does everything to please others. And worst of all, it works! That's not my style. I prefer that others accept me as I am."

Obviously, you don't need to imitate your brother or sister to be accepted, since your personality is just as interesting as theirs, even if you feel that you're sometimes overshadowed by them. If a sibling's personality overwhelms you at times, learn to distance yourself a bit. At home, find a space of your own where you can do something you enjoy, like listening to music or playing on the computer. Go there each time you feel suffocated by your brother or sister's presence. By giving yourself these "alone moments" when you're not comparing yourself to your siblings (or being compared to them by others), you'll start to appreciate your own special qualities.

You can also try asking your friends to meet you outside your house. Spending time with people who appreciate you, who laugh at your jokes, and who think your stories are interesting will build your self-confidence and give you some distance from your siblings.

take care of
yourself!

Conflicts and clashes are normal among people who live together, but family problems can prevent some children from finding a balance in their lives. Some children might be neglected or ignored by one or both parents. That can seriously dent a child's self-esteem.

"If my parents don't give me time or attention," admits Susan, "I feel that it means that I don't count. So I put myself down. What's worse, at certain moments I even hate myself."

Your parents may care very much for you, but find it difficult to show it for a number of reasons. For example, they might be so caught up with work or their own worries that they don't pay much attention to you. Perhaps they were treated with indifference when they were young and don't know any other way of behaving.

"When my parents were twelve, they were already working, like most kids in their country," says Karim. "I would like my parents to be more present in my life. But they see me as an adult and can't look past the cultural differences in their upbringing."

If you feel neglected by your parents—as if you don't matter to them— talk to them about it. Talking about your feelings isn't easy; it takes courage. Think beforehand about what you want to say. Pick a moment when you can be alone with your mother or father—for example, when you're going someplace in the car or preparing dinner together.

Explain in simple terms how you feel. You may want to suggest doing something together, like taking a walk or going on a picnic. It's not easy to start a discussion like this . . . but it's worth it. Your self-esteem will truly

grow when people who are important to you show you love, friendship, and appreciation.

On the other hand, if the people you love ignore you or put you down all the time, you'll start to feel worthless. You'll begin to lose your inner strength and confidence. This is especially true if one of your parents abandons you. A hole develops inside you, like a well that's impossible to fill.

"The compliments people pay me, my good grades, and all my accomplishments aren't enough to give me confidence," Stephanie admits. "I feel handicapped. Instead of lacking an arm or a leg, I lack love."

In this situation, you may need help to reflect upon what you've gone through and how to overcome your problems. A psychologist or other professional can help you see the situation more clearly. They will remind you that you shouldn't blame yourself for who your parents are. Although you might feel that you could have prevented your parent's departure or that you're the reason he or she left, you're wrong: a child is never responsible for the behavior of his or her parents. Professionals can help you recognize that you are worthy of love, respect, and confidence.

family
burdens

Some families have low self-esteem because they've been given a rough ride in life. How can a family possibly maintain a high level of confidence when it suffers from financial problems and can barely afford to pay the bills? How can a family move forward when a parent fears losing his or her job? There's no question that it's difficult to maintain one's confidence in this kind of precarious atmosphere.

For one thing, parents dealing with these problems are often guilty of not giving enough attention to children. In addition, children in these families fear that they'll be abandoned or that there's another crisis waiting around the corner. Sandra, a girl living in this type of situation, says, "I sleep badly at night; I fear that a new catastrophe awaits me in the morning."

Remember this: if your family faces major difficulties, these won't last for eternity, even if it takes a little while to get back on track. Once again,

a person outside the family can help defuse tensions during these difficult moments and make things better for all.

"When my parents separated," says Jenny, "my mother was in such a bad state that she couldn't look after my brothers and me. One of my teachers realized that we needed help. She requested that a teacher come to our house in the afternoons to help us with our homework. The teacher provided the guidance we lacked. It made us feel less alone."

Although you may want to turn to a friend or another family member for help, they may not be qualified. You should never hesitate to ask for professional help when you need it. A psychologist, the school nurse, a teacher, a social worker, and even a telephone hotline for troubled youth are there to help with these kinds of issues. You'll feel less alone, your family problems won't seem so difficult, and little by little you'll build up your confidence and come through in the end.

In all of these instances, try to maintain some distance from the family problems so you won't feel overburdened by everything happening around you. This is not about selfishness or indifference; it's about taking care of yourself.

One way of maintaining some distance is to spend time with friends and classmates whom you trust. Don't seek out the company of those who are also hurting. At first, it may seem helpful to discuss one another's problems together—to take comfort in being victims. But sadness, like joy, is contagious, so you should try to surround yourself with friends who are upbeat and will help you put your family problems in perspective.

one of these families is
not like the other

Some kids feel that their family is so burdened by troubles and so different from other families that they must hide any problems. This happens for different reasons. For example, when Claudia's father started drinking too much, she was afraid that he would become violent in front of other people. Jimmy avoided inviting friends to his house because they reacted strangely when they saw his handicapped brother. Eloise never talks about the fact that she spends her vacations at home because of financial problems.

If you also find it difficult to accept your family's situation, you undoubtedly put yourself down and suffer from shame. "It's hard to talk about my home life," says Salma. "People view my family with contempt. As a result, I prefer to hide."

But just because you or your family have particular problems, that doesn't mean you're nobody! In fact, the difficulties you face on a daily basis will make you stronger. They may force you to grow up faster. You will learn to accept people's differences, adapt to any situation, and develop the ability to handle problems. You will end up with a better understanding of people and their emotions. In time, you'll become less fragile and more open-minded. You will see that when you don't act defensive about your family problems, people will be more at ease in your company.

gain self-confidence with the help of

your loved ones

I'm most comfortable when I'm surrounded by my friends and loved ones; I talk more and express what I truly feel. I know that my parents trust me, and this helps me feel more confident in myself. My parents don't see me as a little kid anymore. They give me more and more freedom as well as responsibilities. For example: I've always loved going shopping. At first, when I left my neighborhood to spend the afternoon in town, my mother was nervous. She called me every hour. Then she began to have more faith in me. It helped me a great deal.

—Maria

putting
the changes
to work

good days
and bad

speaking up in
the classroom

ME AND
OTHERS

dare to be different

happy together?

happy together?

It's around others that you feel your lack of self-esteem the most. You're scared of being judged and criticized, so you may feel you have to behave differently. You smile, even though you don't feel like it; you pretend to be distant, even though you'd rather be close enough to talk honestly; you say someone is right when secretly you disagree with him or her.

It's normal to want to project a good image of yourself. Who doesn't? But if you constantly dwell on how you are perceived by others, you'll find it hard to stand up for yourself or to do things that you might enjoy.

For example, Scott remembers, "A few months ago, I was looking forward to attending my family reunion, where I would see many of my cousins whom I like. I decided not to go at the last minute. I feared that I couldn't compete with them and that I would look stupid."

If you're anxious about the idea of spending time with others, you probably prefer hiding out in your room. It's fine to do this once in a while, but it's important not to isolate yourself all the time. After all, what do you do when you're sad, happy, or filled with wonder? Sooner or later, you will want to share what you feel and experience with other people and exchange ideas, questions, laughs, and sorrows with them.

In fact, everyone needs a balance between time spent alone and time spent with others. When you're alone you can think about yourself, process what you've experienced, empty your mind, and daydream. When you're with others, you become more aware of who you are and what you think. You listen to others' opinions and perhaps rethink some of your own. You feel recognized and understood.

ph3

"For me, friends are essential," explains Judith. "When I have a problem, I know I can talk to them about it. They relate to me when I talk about my concerns regarding school or other friends." What a relief to know that your friends have encountered the same problems as you; somehow, just knowing that other people understand your problems makes these difficulties seem smaller and easier to overcome. When you discuss issues with your friends, you become more aware of the way you think and you might discover aspects about yourself that you didn't think about before. You might even emerge enriched with new ideas.

good days
and bad

When you're feeling down, you attach more importance to other people's impressions of you. Some days you feel vulnerable even before you get out of bed. Or you start doubting yourself the moment you run into people: a word, look, or attitude can shatter your self-confidence. "The other day, two of my classmates made fun of me, saying that I dressed funny," Jasmine says. "I blushed and mumbled something in response. I felt so fragile, like I wanted to hide. I feel like I'm the only person who suffers like this. I hate it and wish I were stronger."

It's tough feeling so vulnerable. You would like to be different. But if some comments hurt you, it just proves that you're a sensitive person,

and that's not a negative. In fact, sensitivity helps you understand others, which is a wonderful quality.

However, you need to keep this in balance. Try not to be *over*sensitive. Avoid paying too much attention to what others say. Tell yourself that their opinions are not necessarily more valuable than your own. They, too, can be wrong. When you have more confidence in your own opinions, you'll be less affected by what others say to you.

On days when you feel particularly sensitive, seek out people who know you well and with whom you feel particularly at ease. Some people are generally enthusiastic and recognize others' self-worth. It is in their company that you will feel most confident.

Of course, some people have a completely different attitude. They show off and talk about their own experiences instead of listening to those of others. Try to distance yourself from these types—they may do you more harm than good. If it's impossible to avoid them, just remember that they act this way because they suffer from self-doubt and have a strong need to feel accepted.

Remember, life isn't a long, tranquil river—not for you and not for anyone else. Though sometimes the waters can be calm, other times they are raging. Everybody confronts both good and bad conditions along the way; the point is to develop enough inner strength to deal with whatever life throws at you.

feeling shy

Shyness is a common problem, but some people are so shy that their anxiety gets in the way of living a full life. "When my family moved when I was twelve, I lost my friends and my bearings," Joyce remembers. "One day at my new school, I started to feel extreme discomfort; my hands started to sweat, my heartbeat quickened, and I started trembling all over."

Kids who react this way don't believe in themselves. They think they count less than other people. They are withdrawn, have trouble communicating, and fear being judged and criticized to such a degree that they try to avoid ever meeting a new person.

Sometimes this reaction is caused by shyness, other times it's due to social phobia. If you have a tendency to remain on the sidelines and refrain from speaking in front of a group, it's a sign of shyness. You can ease your suffering by developing more confidence in yourself.

On the other hand, if you are so anxiety-prone that you avoid all new people or new situations, and feel deep discomfort when faced with them, you most likely suffer from social phobia. People with social phobia become anxious when they have to express their point of view, ask directions from a stranger, practice a sport in front of others, return an item to a store, or take an exam.

If you constantly avoid these kinds of situations out of deep anxiety or even panic, ask your school nurse to refer you to a therapist who specializes in this kind of problem. He or she will help you overcome your fears by teaching you to communicate better, assert yourself, and accept who you are—with your strengths and weaknesses alike.

relationships

with others are not always perfect!

When you're among close friends and loved ones, few words are necessary to express yourself and feel understood. You trust these people more than anyone. Generally speaking, however, relationships with others are very complex and can test your self-confidence.

When several people get together, their conversation can sometimes take the form of a sporting event, with some people trying to dominate and win. Everyone uses his or her own method of getting the upper hand— flattery, aggression, or teasing. If you have high self-esteem, you undoubtedly know how best to assert yourself. Others can't prevent you from taking your place in a discussion.

On the other hand, if you have low self-esteem, other people's asser-tiveness can catch you off guard so that you can't think properly. You may withdraw from the discussion without uttering a word or blush when someone asks you a question. Or you may sound defensive or become more aggressive as a way of hiding your fears.

To learn how to be more comfortable in these situations, start practic-ing with people you trust. Every chance you get, try to express your thoughts and feelings. Then listen to what others have to say and compare them. You might discover that you enjoy speaking and listening to others after all.

Next, take what you've learned and apply it to a bigger group, or to people you don't know as well. Take part in the discussion without dominat-ing it. Seek out classmates or adults who don't resort to criticism or mock-ery. You'll find that more often than not, you'll enjoy the discussion.

At times, you might be disappointed. You might feel that you didn't express yourself well or that other people didn't understand what you were trying to say. That's normal. It doesn't take much for a conversation to go

off track; the other person might be worried, impatient, nervous, or tired. Don't be discouraged! The circumstances will likely be different the next time and the discussion will go more smoothly.

dare to be
different

𝒩ow that you've gained more confidence in yourself, you like offering your point of view and even daring to disagree with others. But that means you also risk annoying, or even angering, other people because not all people believe the same things.

This can be upsetting if your self-confidence is still a bit shaky, since your fear of criticism and rejection is still quite strong. If you find yourself in an argument, try explaining yourself calmly, without either becoming too aggressive or withdrawing completely from the conversation. You'll be surprised by how much people appreciate those who express themselves calmly and sincerely.

In addition, learn to listen to others' opinions; you'll become more open-minded and understanding as a result. Reality, you'll discover, can be perceived in a number of ways. There need not be a right or wrong opinion.

Of course, this doesn't mean that you should be argumentative each time someone holds a contrary opinion. In some circumstances, it might be better to give in, in order to avoid a useless conflict. For example, if you disagree with a teacher, it's up to you to decide when to keep arguing a point, and when to keep quiet. When you've learned how to successfully make this choice, you'll know that you've mastered the art of listening to yourself and others.

speaking up in the
classroom

Sometimes, you have no choice: you have to face certain situations, even if you'd prefer to be ten miles underground! One of these situations is public speaking. You're standing in front of your class, everyone else is seated, and all eyes are on you; you anxiously await the question you'll be asked, or the subject you will have to discuss. Your heart is beating out of your chest, you feel like you've forgotten everything you've learned, and that you'll never be able to give the right answer. Fortunately, there are a couple of exercises you can practice that will help in stressful situations.

For example, have you ever noticed that you experience shortness of breath in these situations? It feels like your ribcage is stifling your breath and preventing you from breathing normally.

To avoid this, try to concentrate on your breathing. Several minutes before you're asked to speak, place a hand on your stomach and breathe normally. Inhale, letting the air enter your lungs and lightly push your stomach out. Then exhale gently, allowing your stomach to resume its initial position.

It's worth practicing this once in a while on your own. Try it when you're sitting at your desk or lying on your bed. You can even try it when you're riding in the car or on a bus, or waiting in line at the store. When you concentrate on your breathing, your stress levels fall and you soon find an inner calm. Your thoughts will become clearer: steady in-and-out breathing promotes creativity. (It's no wonder that the word "inspiration" is used to describe both the act of drawing air into your lungs *and* the formulation of new ideas in your mind.)

There is another simple and effective exercise you can do before a presentation or any other activity that makes you nervous: go to a quiet place, close your eyes, and imagine the situation that frightens you, but visualize it unfolding in a positive way.

For example, if you have to give a report, imagine yourself standing in front of the class, poised and calm. Imagine that you forget that people are watching you because you're so focused on your topic. Imagine that you enjoy having everyone listen to what you have to say. By visualizing this scene at night in bed, you will sleep more soundly and wake up feeling more confident. You'll face your day feeling great and ready to do your best.

But don't forget to prepare for the big event! Some people are so afraid of speaking in front of a group that they conveniently forget to get ready for it. Don't count on improvisation—it will probably backfire. When you feel that you've mastered your presentation, ask some of your classmates to practice with you. Think about trick questions that could catch you off guard. Preparation is a good way to maintain control; it will help you be more sure of yourself at the important moment.

putting the changes
to work

When you take time to work on your self-confidence, you'll soon see changes in yourself. You'll become more open, alert, and spontaneous. And that can change your life in all kinds of ways.

For example, Alexandra says, "One day I was feeling good about myself, so I complimented Julie on her nice haircut. From the look in her eyes, I saw that she was very touched by my comment. Now we hang out together."

If you take advantage of every opportunity to speak up, make new friends, and try new things, your self-esteem will continue to grow. There's an easy explanation for this: the more you assert yourself, the more others will get to know you, appreciate you, and show more interest in you. This will have a snowball effect, increasing your confidence and your ability to appreciate your strengths.

You have so much to gain from opening yourself to others. Your good qualities, which once were stifled, will be given room to develop. With each new day, they'll develop even more. You'll start to appreciate the moments you spend alone, as well as those spent with others. In short, your confidence will continue to grow, helping you throughout your life.

fear of not
measuring up

I often question my academic abilities. My brother is very much at ease in the classroom. He studies less than me, but always gets better grades. I find that unfair. Even when I study a lot, my grades are never as good as his. If I don't understand something the first time around, I start to seriously doubt my intelligence.

I'm never at ease during oral exams, when the teacher is watching and listening to me. If I hesitate or don't know the answer to a question, he notices right away. It feels like I'm being judged, and that throws me off balance. I fall to pieces. I have trouble concentrating and feel like a nobody. Written exams are different. If I don't know the answer to something right away, I know I can think it through before writing a response. I'm trying to have the same confidence in my oral exams in the future.

—Chad

knowing yourself

Do you know which situations make you lose your self-confidence? And do you know when you feel sure of yourself and ready to take on anything?

Here's one last test that will help you think more about your behavior and attitudes toward yourself, family, and friends.

For each subject, read the choices and pick the one that best matches your way of thinking. If you're stuck between two choices, ask yourself the question in a different way: "Do I have a tendency to . . . "

The point is to try to better understand yourself and your reactions to various situations. Keep working on the exercises in this book and take the test again in a year—you may find that you've changed a lot more than you thought!

self-confidence
checklist

Me

- ❏ I am unaware of my strengths
- ❏ I feel like a failure
- ❏ I tend to play down my accomplishments
- ❏ I'm too cautious
- ❏ I don't feel good about my body
- ❏ I would like to be different
- ❏ I can't make decisions
- ❏ I don't like change

Me and Others

- ❏ I prefer to keep quiet and listen to others
- ❏ I don't like criticism
- ❏ I don't like to compete
- ❏ I don't know what others see in me
- ❏ I keep my opinions to myself
- ❏ I don't feel accepted by others
- ❏ Compliments make me uncomfortable

- ❏ I can write a list of my strengths
- ❏ I can succeed
- ❏ I'm proud of my accomplishments
- ❏ I take risks
- ❏ I feel good about my body
- ❏ I accept myself the way I am
- ❏ I like making decisions
- ❏ I like experiencing new things

- ❏ I like speaking in front of a group
- ❏ I accept criticism and try to learn from it
- ❏ Competition motivates me
- ❏ I'm aware of my positive traits
- ❏ I have no problem saying what I think
- ❏ I feel accepted by others
- ❏ I enjoy getting complimented

ph3

Me and School

- ❏ I doubt my academic abilities
- ❏ I feel nervous when I'm questioned in class
- ❏ I get scared before exams, even if I'm prepared
- ❏ I avoid getting called on and don't ask questions
- ❏ I have trouble finding my place among my classmates
- ❏ I control everything I say
- ❏ I'm afraid of being criticized
- ❏ I feel overlooked

- ❏ I believe in my academic abilities
- ❏ I welcome questions in class
- ❏ I feel confident before taking an exam
- ❏ I actively participate in class discussions
- ❏ I'm at ease with my classmates
- ❏ I am spontaneous
- ❏ Criticism doesn't bother me
- ❏ I am comfortable as the center of attention

index

Marie-José Auderset spent years as a radio journalist and now writes principally about current issues.

N. B. Grace is a *New York Times* bestselling author. She lives in New York City.